Keiko's Story

The real-life tale of the world's most famous killer whale.

By Diane Coplin Hammond • Illustrated by Nyna Somerville

Peduncle
Press,
Inc.

ISBN 0-9665778-1-7

Library of Congress Catalog Card Number 98-67379

Peduncle Press
P.O. Box 846
Waldport, OR
97394
peduncle@fbo.com

To Keiko, who's shown the way,
and to the people at the Free Willy Keiko Foundation,
who've had the courage to follow.

In late 1977 or early 1978 a young killer whale was
born in the gray North Atlantic off the shores of
Iceland. Thousands of killer whales live in
these broad, cold seas. The young
whale's name was Kago.
You may know him as Keiko.

For two years Keiko stayed close to his relatives in a tight family group called a pod. The whales followed salmon, herring and other tasty fish, eating and playing and talking together by squeaks and whistles and clicks.

Perhaps by then Keiko had mastered how to hunt and eat without the help of an adult whale.

Perhaps he was still learning from them. No one knows for sure.

What we do know is that in 1979, when Keiko was about
two years old, he swam into a net near a fishing boat.
The people who caught him wanted to send him to an
aquarium or marine park where others could see
him and learn about killer whales. He was
still less than 10 feet long—smaller than
two six-year-olds lying head to toe.

At first there were no buyers, so for three years Keiko stayed in a holding pool in Iceland. Then he was sold to Marineland in Canada and took his first airplane ride. He traveled in a big waterproof box filled with cold water, and his doctor kept him company on the way. He was a calm and patient traveler.

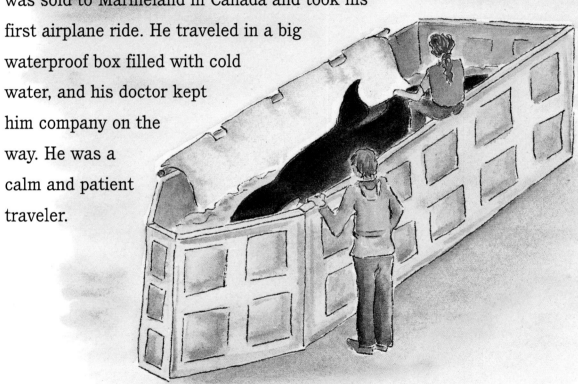

At Marineland Keiko lived with other killer whales and began his formal training. He learned to jump from the water when he was asked, splashing down, entering head-first or landing on his back. Killer whales do these things in the wild. At Marineland he did them during shows.

But Keiko was the smallest, youngest killer whale and the other whales were bossy. Keiko just didn't fit in, so two years later he was sold again, this time to Reino Aventura in Mexico.

There, his name was changed from
Kago to Keiko. He performed in
shows there, too, and was dearly
loved by the children of Mexico. He
was the only killer whale in all of Central
America and shared his pool with bottlenose
dolphins. Three of the dolphins were called Lilly,
Pepe and Richie, and they often played with their
much larger pool-mate. Sometimes Keiko swam
around the pool wearing two dolphins on
his head like a hat.

But there, too, life became difficult for Keiko. Because Mexico City is far from the ocean, his pool couldn't be filled with natural sea water. And the park couldn't afford to keep the water cold, so in summer the temperature got way too warm. This made Keiko sluggish and slow, and when he wasn't doing his daily shows he floated at the top of the water like a log.

Keiko kept his back out of the
water so much that his boneless
dorsal fin had nothing to hold
it up. He also swam around
his pool in only one
direction, so bit by bit
his fin leaned more to
one side than the other.

Pretty soon it began to
droop and curl until it
nearly touched his back.
This sometimes happens to
wild killer whales, too.
Luckily, it doesn't hurt.

The worst thing was that Keiko's Mexican pool began to seem smaller and smaller. As he grew from a 10-foot whale to nearly 20 feet long he became weak because there was no room to exercise.

The food he ate wasn't always enough, so gradually he became very thin. He also had a virus that gave him sores like warts on his pectoral flippers and tail. These would get better sometimes, but they never really went away.

Many people worked with Keiko in Mexico, and they loved his easy nature and gentle ways. Because they loved him, they worried a great deal about his health. They knew his pool had become too small, and his sores needed to heal. But they had no way to make his pool bigger, or to bring him the fresh cold sea water that might help him get well.

So one day Keiko's Mexican owners decided something very difficult: they decided that although the people of Mexico would miss him terribly, they must find him a better home.

In the meantime the world's children met Keiko in the movie *Free Willy*, and like the children of Mexico they quickly grew to love him. When they learned that he was sick they sent money and letters to help. In fact, so many people cared about Keiko that millions of dollars were raised.

Just before Christmas 1994, Keiko's owners gave him to the Free Willy Keiko Foundation and a brand-new pool was built just for him at the Oregon Coast Aquarium.

Newport, Oregon

Mexico City

At midnight on January 7, 1996, Keiko swam into a stretcher, was lifted from his Mexican pool and was put into a box of icy cold water—just the right temperature for a traveling killer whale. Many thousands of Mexican men, women and children lined the streets to say goodbye as Keiko began his long journey to the United States.

Twenty hours later, with great pride, the United Parcel Service delivered him safely to his new Oregon home.

Keiko was stiff and sore after his trip, the way people sometimes feel after a long car ride. At first he didn't swim or explore very much, even though his new pool was four times bigger than the one he had left behind in Mexico. But in two or three days he began swimming everywhere, investigating the rocky hills and caves on the bottom of the pool and looking through the big underwater windows at his visitors. Children interested him most, and he often picked them instead of grown-ups to watch.

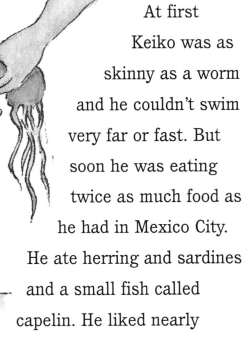

At first Keiko was as skinny as a worm and he couldn't swim very far or fast. But soon he was eating twice as much food as he had in Mexico City. He ate herring and sardines and a small fish called capelin. He liked nearly everything offered but squid. The first time he was given the slippery stuff, he stopped eating and swam around the pool slapping his tail on the water in annoyance. His American caretakers gently insisted because squid was so good for him, and soon he ate it without complaint—unless he was rather full, and then he might still spit it out.

After just four months in his new Oregon
home Keiko's huge warts were all gone, every
one. For the first time in 12 years he could move
his pectoral flippers easily because nothing hurt
and nothing got in the way. He was getting fat, too.
And because he was feeling better, he had a lot more
energy to burn. So he began to make up games. At
first they were simple games, like swimming with
his tongue hanging out of the side of his mouth
and waggling his pectoral flippers. Sometimes
he looked pretty silly.

Then he was ready for more complicated games. He was given a blue plastic ball, his first toy in Oregon. He didn't know how to play with it, but his trainers taught him step by step.

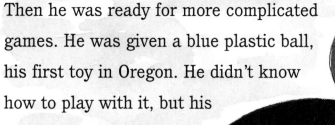

He learned to push the ball with his nose, and balance it on his head, and swim with it completely underwater. One day he even taught himself to jump with the ball on the end of his nose.

Keiko soon got other toys in different shapes and sizes, and invented more and more ways to play. He was learning something very important. He was learning that being Keiko could be fun.

Eight people now take care of Keiko. They feed him, pet him, play with him and cheer when he does things well. They encourage him to exercise, and invent new games so he won't get bored.

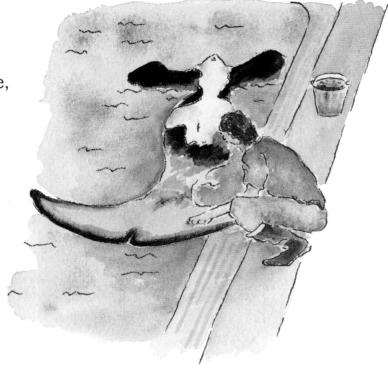

They all say the same thing: because of his gentle and easy-going ways, Keiko is a one in a million whale. As in Mexico, Keiko is surrounded by people who love him.

Much has changed for Keiko since his first blustery days in Oregon. He no longer performs in shows. He is fatter, peppier, stronger and more curious. None of his sores have come back, and he has grown more than one foot longer. He has learned how to chase, catch and eat live fish instead of eating only dead ones.

Best of all, he has begun to understand that he can make choices and think for himself. These things are fun, and one day they may help him survive in the wild.

The people who own Keiko have made him a promise. They will take him back home to his Icelandic waters, and the men and women who care for him will all be going, too. At first he will stay in a pen made of nets, safe while he gets used to living with nature. The sea is a noisy place and he will hear the sounds of animals all around him, like small crabs and fish, like big seals and killer whales.

The rest of Keiko's promise is this: if he can communicate well with other killer whales and hunt for food on his own, he may live in the wild once again. But if he cannot, he will always be cared for—at home, in the sea, in Iceland.

There are many questions to answer before we know how Keiko's story will end. But we do know one thing: Keiko will always be loved. He will be loved by those who've cared for him, by those who've traveled far to see him, and by the children of the world who, by caring so much, have helped give Keiko a second chance to be healthy and free.